LOST

Written by **Dennis B. Harris**

Edited by **Lana Kay Harris**

Illustrated by **Lee Herring**

ISBN 1-890022-00-4

Dedication

First, to the Lord Jesus Christ, who loved us enough to die for us, and without whom this book would be pointless.

To the children who will read this book and to those who will have it read to them.

To Kim, Mat and Heather, and Mike. Without whom my life would be meaningless and this series of books would have been impossible.

To my little ballerina…my light and my air.

To Ron, who is teaching my little ballerina to know the voice of God.

Finally to Kay, without whose support and faith, this book would still be in the word processor. You are proof that Angels really do exist.

"I am come to seek and to save that which was lost"
Luke 19:10

Bobby was so happy that his dad had decided to take him on the hunting trip to Colorado. He had studied hard and was a very safe hunter. His dad's decision made him feel as though he was one of the "big guys". He could hardly wait until that big day.

Dad and Uncle Josh would pick him up after school on Friday afternoon.

"All my friends will see me get in the car to go hunting," thought Bobby.

That night he dreamed about the campfire, the tent and the mountain streams.

Bobby could even taste the bacon and eggs his dad would make every morning. Everything tasted better when you were camping.

Then the big day was here. Bobby got up extra early because he had to help get things ready before school.

He gathered up his hunting clothes and his new boots that his dad had gotten him for walking in the mountains. He took all of his hunting gear to the garage.

WOW!! Look at all that stuff. There was a great big tent, sleeping bags, big black pots to cook in and a real cowboy coffee pot.

This was going to be a great trip!

That day at school, Bobby had a hard time paying attention. He kept drifting off to the pine trees and the cool streams.

The clouds outside the classroom window all looked like snow covered mountains.

……"divided by 41, Bobby……BOBBY!" said Miss Wilson. "Are you daydreaming again?"

"Sorry, Miss Wilson," said Bobby.

R-I-N-N-N-N-N-N-N-G! Saved by the bell! YAHOOOOO!!!!

This had been the longest day in the history of school. Bobby couldn't get outside fast enough.

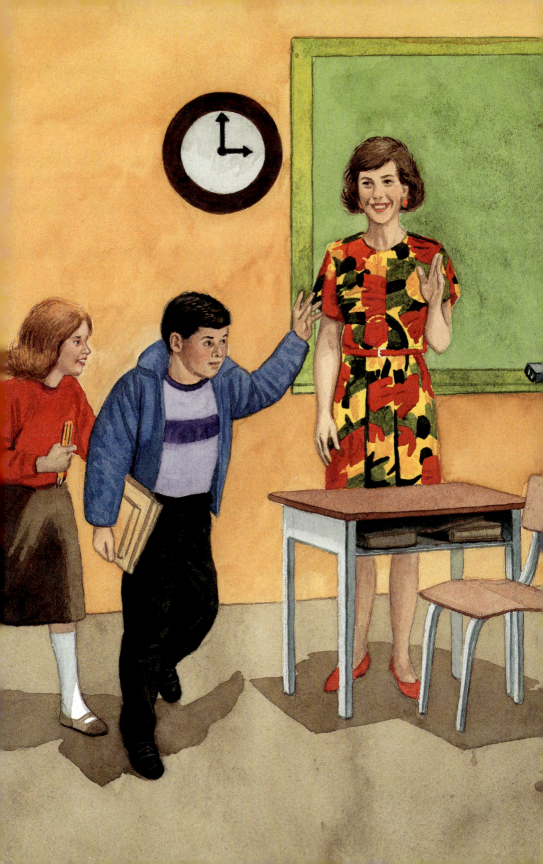

His friends all gathered around the car to wish him good luck. He felt like the luckiest kid in the world.

"Ready, Bobby? Let's go…!" said Uncle Josh.

It would take all night to get there, but Bobby didn't mind. They would play travel games and look for wildlife along the way. He really enjoyed that special time with his dad.

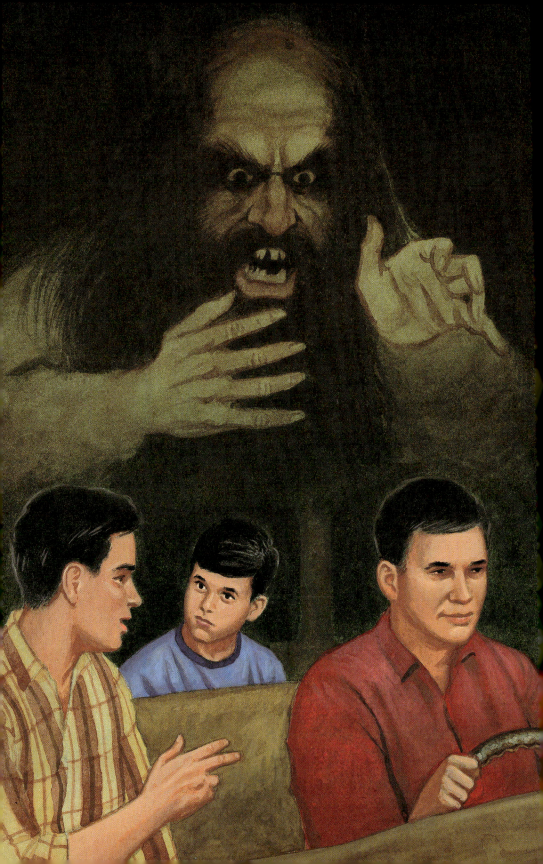

In the middle of the night, Uncle Josh began to tell scary stories about "El Choclo".

"Who is El Choclo?" exclaimed Bobby.

"El Choclo looks for boys when they get too far away from the campfire or when they make too much noise in the woods," teased Uncle Josh.

"Are you teasing me?" hoped Bobby.

"You better get some sleep. It's going to be a big day tomorrow," chuckled Dad.

Bobby was almost sure they were teasing him, but as he tried to sleep, he decided to keep one eye open, just in case.

Before Bobby knew it, he was awakened by the sun shining in the car window.

He could see the purple outline of the mountains as they got closer.

He began to get more and more excited!

Around the curves and up the steep mountain they went. Bobby could see way down the mountain from the window on his side of the car.

When they finally arrived, it was the most beautiful camping spot he had ever seen. The air was so clean and cool. The trees were green and so tall, it looked like they could almost touch the clouds.

He could hear the leaves as they whispered in the wind.

First, the big yellow tent went up.

It was funny helping with the tent. Neither Dad nor Uncle Josh wanted to read the instructions. Once, Bobby's dad got trapped inside the tent and began yelling. It was really funny.

"Camping is fun, Dad!" said Bobby.

"Sure is," answered Dad.

That afternoon, they went hiking. They walked up, down, and all around the mountain.

They talked about the animals they saw and tried to name the trees and the flowers.

When they got back to camp, Dad made a fireplace of rocks. It was Bobby's job to gather wood.

Later that evening, after dinner, they sat around the campfire roasting marshmallows and singing songs.

Uncle Josh started another scary story about "El Choclo".

They had a great time.

The next morning while it was still cold and dark, Bobby woke up to the smell of bacon and eggs cooking.

"Better clean your plate, Bobby, it's going to be a long day," said Dad.

"No problem, Dad, I'm starving," said Bobby.

After breakfast, Bobby and his dad began hiking and hunting. They hunted together all morning. It was so much fun to walk along with his dad.

They came to a small stream and decided to stop and eat lunch. "Listen to that squirrel barking," said Dad.

"I know a great hunting spot just over this mountain," said Dad.

And up they went together.

Soon, they came to the side of the mountain where they would hunt. Dad pointed out a big rock and very carefully explained that Bobby was not to leave this rock.

WOW! Bobby was going to get to hunt on his own! He was very happy that his dad trusted him.

Bobby knew he was a safe hunter. He had taken all the safety courses and this was the day. He felt so proud and tall.

"DON'T LEAVE THIS ROCK!" Dad said again. "I will come back to get you just after dark."

"Bobby, pay attention. DON'T LEAVE THIS ROCK! Stay close to it, so I can find you, when I get back!" Dad said, this time very seriously.

Later, after his dad had left, having seen nothing very interesting, Bobby began to look across the hillside to a place that really looked like a better spot. The more he looked, the better the other spot seemed.

"Why couldn't he go over there?" thought Bobby.

"Did Dad *really* say not to *leave* this rock, or did he say not to go so far that I couldn't *see* this rock? After all, the other spot was very close. Surely, he could see the first rock easily from there," reasoned Bobby.

Bobby was right!

He could see the rock from the new spot. It wasn't as big and it looked a little different from this direction, but he could still see it.

Then, he heard a noise! "What was that?" wondered Bobby. "Maybe, it's a big deer. I'll just move a bit further and see what made the sound. After all, it is only a couple of feet further and I can still see this new rock," said Bobby to himself.

At the second new place, he could not hear the noise anymore. So, he decided to go back to the rock he had chosen. That way, he could see where he needed to be when his dad came back at dark. HEY!!!!! Bobby hadn't noticed it was almost dark already. He could barely see the new rock.

Bobby began to hurry to get back to meet his dad. "The big rock… where was it? It was right here just a minute ago. He hadn't gone that far away… had he?" worried Bobby.

It was now completely dark. He didn't know that it got dark faster in the mountains. But, it did.

BOBBY WAS LOST!!!

It was REAL DARK. Bobby thought he could hear something breathing behind him. What was that? Something was walking close to him. Boy, was he scared!

His uncle had told him a story about "El Choclo". Maybe, that was what he heard behind that tree.

Bobby then noticed that it was getting real cold. He began to shiver. He hoped someone would find him before it got much colder.

After what seemed hours that Bobby sat on the cold, dark mountainside, he heard his name being called. "Bobby!" The voice sounded a long way off. "HERE I AM!" cried Bobby.

"Bobby!" The voice was closer and now, he could hear that it was his dad.

"Oh, no," thought Bobby. "I guess I will never get to hunt alone again. Dad is going to punish me for disobeying him. I have been so wrong! I hope Dad can forgive me."

Then, he heard his name again. Now, it was much closer and he could see a light.

"DAD!!!! Here I am," cried Bobby, as he began running toward the light.

"Stand still! I will come to you!" yelled his dad.

"Dad, I am so sorry," cried Bobby. "I thought that…" but, Bobby didn't have time to explain. His dad picked him up and held him close. Bobby thought he saw a tear in his dad's eyes. His dad carried him all the way back to the camp. All the time, Bobby was asking his dad to forgive him and to give him a second chance.

The campfire was warm and his bed seemed extra soft that night.

Bobby's dad had forgiven him. The funny thing was, he didn't even act like he remembered that Bobby had disobeyed him, the next morning.

The next Sunday, his Sunday School teacher, Mr. Sparkman, told him Satan always tries to trick us into disobeying God.

That the Devil always uses a lie to make us doubt what God says. Mr. Sparkman said, the Devil could make sin look safe and fun. He said, the Devil always tries to trick us into leaving the safety of God's love by making it look better or more fun somewhere else.

He explained that Jesus is our Rock and Salvation.

Mr. Sparkman told Bobby that when we disobey God, we get farther away from Him. And, we can get so far away from Him that we can barely hear His voice calling us anymore. He told Bobby that God sent Jesus to find us. He said, Jesus was calling our name and looking everywhere for us.

Mr. Sparkman said that Jesus is the Light of the World and we have to make a choice when we hear Him calling us.

We can either stay where we are and Jesus will walk past us, or we can call out, "Here I am, save me and forgive me for disobeying you".

He said that Jesus loves us so much that He died, so we could be forgiven, forever.

Suddenly, it all became so clear to Bobby. He told Jesus that he loved Him and he wanted Him to come into his heart and to forgive him of his sin.

And, you know what…?

Jesus did it.

If you would like to invite Jesus into your heart like Bobby did, ask your parents or your pastor to pray this simple prayer with you.

"Dear Jesus, thank you for loving me enough to die for me. Forgive me for disobeying you and please save me. I believe you are God's only son and I invite you to be my Lord. In Jesus' name, Amen."

"…Rejoice with me, for I have found my sheep which was lost!" Luke 15:6

"For God so loved the World, that He gave His only begotten Son, that whosoever believed in Him, would not perish, but have everlasting life." John 3:16